By Paula N. Kessler

Illustrations by J. J. Smith-Moore

RANDOM HOUSE 🏠 NEW YORK

To my parents, who are my friends—P. N. K.

Copyright © 1995 by RGA Publishing Group, Inc.
Illustrations copyright © 1995 by J. J. Smith-Moore
Cover photograph: J. Feingersh/The Stock Market

Library of Congress Cataloging-in-Publication Data

Kessler, Paula N.
    Amazing kids! / by Paula N. Kessler ; illustrated by J. J. Smith-Moore.
       p. cm. — (Kidbacks)
    ISBN 0-679-86943-3
    1. Children—United States—Biography—Juvenile literature.
    2. Social action—United States—Case studies—Juvenile literature.
    3. Success—United States—Case studies—Juvenile literature.
    4. Children as volunteers—United States—Case studies—Juvenile
    literature. [1. Biography. 2. Social action. 3. Success.
    4. Voluntarism.]
    I. J. J. Smith-Moore, ill. II. Title. III. Series.
    HQ792.U5K47 1994
    305.23'0973—dc20   94-28961

Manufactured in the United States of America
10 9 8 7 6 5 4 3 2 1
KIDBACKS is a trademark of Random House, Inc.

CONTENTS

PREFACE
BEFORE YOU BEGIN

Amazing Kids! **is a family of inspiring stories about courage and dedication,** about growing and giving. The stories span environmental issues, the arts, sports, community service, adventure, learning, and much more. The book is about kids taking what they care about, what they're curious about, what they enjoy, and sharing it with others.

These kids have seen and experienced so many different things. They come from large cities and small towns. Some were born in other countries. Some go to school, others learn at home. Some have large families, others are only children. They are from all walks of life. And though each kid is unique, they seem to have some things in common. They have taken their ideas and turned them into actions. They have taken their abilities and talents and turned them into achievements. They've taken their beliefs and concerns and made things happen. They've taken what's inside of them and let it out.

Because of kids, homeless people are eating home-cooked meals in Dallas. In New Jersey, underprivileged boys are riding the first bikes they have ever owned. Sea turtles are being protected in Florida. Kentucky has its first-ever black history course in the public high schools. And the water is safer to drink in North Carolina. Kids are doing all sorts of things.

What a joy it's been for me to write this book. I feel as if I've been on a wonderful journey that's offered windows into some very special young lives. I am truly in awe of these amazing kids and am very excited to share their stories with you.

—PAULA N. KESSLER

5

TEDDY ANDREWS

SAY YAY!

When Teddy Andrews was seven years old, his mother decided that it was time for him to learn about civics. She took him to a meeting with a local politician, hoping Teddy would learn something about politics and about understanding people's rights. Teddy would rather have played with his friends or done just about anything else. But in spite of his early resistance, it didn't take long before Teddy really *did* become interested and get involved. He joined the campaign for Donald Jelinek, a politician running for city council in Berkeley, California. Teddy liked Jelinek's politics because Jelinek was very interested in helping the homeless.

> "Help people whenever you can, because someday you may need that same help, and you'll want someone to be there for you."

Teddy worked hard for Jelinek, going door to door, urging people to vote for him. Teddy hung posters, ran errands, and did whatever else was needed for the campaign. Jelinek won the election, and an elated Teddy, still only seven years old, asked to be appointed to the Berkeley Youth Commission, a group that focuses on the needs of youth in the community.

Although Teddy knew that you didn't have to be twenty-one years old to join the group, there had never *been* a youth on the Berkeley Youth Commission before. Jelinek thought it was time for that to change. So he chose Teddy as the first-ever *youth* to be the Berkeley Youth Commissioner. Every day after school for an entire year, Teddy campaigned for homeless kids, developed special parks-and-recreation programs on their behalf, and identified other projects for needy children. After a year, Jelinek's term expired, and so did Teddy's job as commissioner. But Teddy's work didn't end there.

As Berkeley Youth Commissioner, Teddy had noticed that there were no other kids on local boards or committees, and he felt that was unfair. He believed that kids were not getting their point of view expressed. To Teddy, this was age discrimination and completely unfair.

So Teddy founded SAY YAY!, Save American Youth, Youth Advocates for Youth. SAY YAY! distributes free school supplies to homeless kids, holds toy drives, and helps create and staff learning centers throughout Berkeley and Oakland for homeless and needy children. Members

even provide a baby-sitting service for grandparents who are raising their grandchildren. Members also founded a twenty-four-hour SAY YAY! children's shelter for homeless kids.

"We contemplate projects and put them into motion," says Teddy. "I only get frustrated because there is so much to do and we can't do it all."

There are more than 400 SAY YAY! volunteers in the Berkeley area, most of whom are under fourteen. "As long as a kid can express himself and talk, he can help," says Teddy. There are members as young as five years old. Some adults also volunteer, says Teddy. "We need them around to do the legal work."

Teddy was the youngest politician in the United States when he was the Berkeley Youth Commissioner. He took his political position seriously, caring for others and looking out for those in need. But Teddy had learned about caring for people many years before. "I learned from my mom about helping people, and I've always been around people who care about others," says Teddy. "It's nice knowing that I've helped too."

Teddy's advice to kids: "Help people whenever you can, because someday you may need that same help, and you'll want someone to be there for you."

KRISTEN BELANGER
FROM HER HEART TO THEIR SOULS

Kristen Belanger knows about poverty, hunger, and homelessness—not only from television or from the newspapers, but from her personal experience working with people less fortunate than herself. Kristen lives in Woodbury, Connecticut, and she is lucky. She isn't poor, hungry, or homeless, but she was taught from a young age about giving and caring for other people.

Kristen is an advocate for people in need, whether they're hungry, homeless, or just lonely. She takes initiative and is very persistent. When she was nine years old, Kristen's family had an open Thanksgiving for people who had nowhere to go and nothing to eat. It made sense to her and her family to share what they had with others.

By the time Kristen was ten, she had already held a food drive to

help supply a local soup kitchen. She had organized a clothing drive, sending nearly half a ton of clothing to an Indian reservation in South Dakota. And she had collected and distributed thousands of toys and hundreds of children's books to homeless shelters and poor families.

"These are people who need the same stuff as us," Kristen says. "They're just like us, but they don't have nice houses and warm beds, or even warm clothes."

Now, at twelve, Kristen is still raising money, collecting clothing, and brainstorming ways to help. She constantly tries to learn all she can about her community, its people in need, and the organizations that might be helpful to them. When she comes up with an idea or sees a need in her community, Kristen writes dozens of letters to business owners, city officials, and newspapers, looking for support. She's learned that usually 10 percent of the people to whom she writes will indeed respond *and* help.

> **"Now that I know what I know, and have seen what I have seen, I will never stop helping others. If I stop now, I'll be letting people down and letting myself down."**

In 1994, when Kristen began organizing her yearly community Easter celebration, she asked the local food bank to supply her with a list of needy kids in the area. She also got a toy store to donate hundreds of dollars' worth of toys. She convinced people and businesses in her community to contribute, organize, and volunteer at the event. Hundreds of needy kids attended the party. They ate wonderful food, had an Easter egg hunt, and played with new toys that they could keep.

Kristen's latest clothing drive was a particularly rewarding experience. More than 1,500 pounds of clothing were collected, and Kristen decided to take the clothes to the Indian reservation herself.

"When I went to South Dakota, I saw the people waiting for the trucks of clothing," said Kristen. "I got such a good feeling to hand a kid a sweater when it was four degrees out and he had on only a T-shirt. It was incredible."

Kristen has every intention of continuing her extensive volunteer work. She considers her parents her role models. They have been very supportive of her work, joining in whenever they can.

"They have always been activists and have followed through on things that they believe in," says Kristen.

Kristen has recently started speaking to kids at schools, teaching them how to develop their *own* projects to benefit others. She believes people first need to understand the conditions under which many others live, because once people understand, they will want to get involved.

"Now that I know what I know, and have seen what I have seen," says Kristen, "I will never stop helping others. If I stop now, I'll be letting people down and letting myself down."

TAKE ACTION!

Take some initiative and do something for the benefit of others, such as organizing a food drive or collecting unwanted clothing to give to those who are in need. Your drive can be simple, with just you and your friends going around the neighborhood asking for donations. Or you can do it on a larger scale by encouraging your whole school to become involved.

DARYL BERNSTEIN

FULL OF IDEAS

When Daryl Bernstein was eight years old, he did what many eight-year-old kids do. Daryl made some lemonade, gathered together cups and straws, made a sign, and walked down the driveway to the curb to set up his first lemonade stand. Daryl had made enough lemonade to serve forty customers. He was already thinking of ways to spend the ten-plus dollars he was going to make.

One problem. Daryl had only two customers—his mother and father. But instead of giving up, Daryl got thinking. There must be *something* a kid could do that would provide a service people were willing to pay for. But what?

Nine years and two published books later, Daryl (now seventeen) has thought of *many* just such enterprises. In his 1992 book *Better Than a Lemonade Stand: Small Business Ideas for Kids,* and 1993's *Kids Can Succeed: 51 Tips for Real Life from One Kid to Another,* Daryl has not only come up with all the ideas he's written about, but he has *tried* each one himself.

"I hope not to have a job per se, but more of an adventure."

"The ideas come from everywhere," Daryl says, "but mainly from wandering around my neighborhood and noticing things that need attention . . . things that might not be very obvious." For example, several years ago Daryl noticed that the newspaper carriers in his Scottsdale, Arizona, neighborhood left the newspapers they delivered at the end of people's driveways. Some of those driveways were very steep, and it occurred to Daryl that people might really appreciate, and even pay, someone to carry their newspapers up to their front doors. He was right. Not only did he make money doing just this, but he got to know his neighbors—many of whom would become customers for *future* business ventures.

Daryl enjoys sharing what he has learned with other kids. "It is really rewarding to see kids reading my books and getting something out of it," he says. "Sometimes they share their own ideas, too." His books suggest small businesses for kids to start, and also include tips on how to get along with your parents, how to develop better homework habits, and how to separate work from free time. "When you separate your work from your play, you get your work done faster and enjoy your free time more," Daryl says.

Besides writing books and attending high school, Daryl has two businesses: a computer-aided graphics design company, in which he designs logos, letterheads, and business cards, and a house-sitting business to care for neighbors' homes when they are out of town.

Daryl's dream is to be wildly successful as an entrepreneur. "I hope not to have a job per se," he says, "but more of an adventure." Last year Daryl was flown to Switzerland to receive a Global Leader for Tomorrow Award at the World Economic Forum. The award recognizes future leaders who were born after 1950. He was the youngest person to be so honored.

DWAINA BROOKS

FEEDING THE HOMELESS

Every morning on her way to school, Dwaina Brooks walked by a line of men and women outside a homeless shelter in her hometown of Dallas, Texas. Many of them looked cold and completely worn out. Dwaina noticed that no one ever stopped to talk to these people. They just passed them by.

In school, her fourth-grade class was doing a unit on homelessness. Every week students would call a homeless shelter and talk with someone who was staying there. Dwaina had heard lots of stories. Most people's lives had been going along okay until something had happened. Whether they had lost their jobs or gotten sick, or their family had split up, the result was often the same—they didn't have any money for food or rent, and they had lost their homes.

> **"There isn't a one of us who hasn't been helped by someone else."**

One day on her way home from school Dwaina stopped to talk to a homeless man. "What do you need?" she asked him.

"I need a job and a home," he said. Dwaina didn't know how she could get him either of those things, so she asked if there was anything else that he needed.

"I'd love a really good meal," the man said. It was at that moment that Dwaina realized how she could help.

She went straight home and told her mom about the man and her class unit on the homeless. Dwaina told her that she wanted to make food for the homeless, and her mother agreed that it was a good idea and that she would be willing to help too.

With Dwaina donating her lunch money (three dollars) to the cause, she and her family came up with sixty dollars to spend. That Friday night, after three days of shopping and planning, cutting coupons, and buying discounted meats and day-old bread, Dwaina, her mother, and her two sisters got started. They formed an assembly line and began frying chicken, baking cookies, and making sandwiches. They then placed

TAKE ACTION!

Pick a group of people less fortunate than you and do something to help them. You can help older adults in your neighborhood with their shopping, bring flowers to the sick, or, like Dwaina, make food for a homeless shelter. Your help and support will be greatly appreciated and will make you feel really good.

each meal in a box donated by a local baker. By ten that evening, they had made more than one hundred meals, which they drove immediately to the shelter. Many of the people there were asleep, but they were in for a treat the next morning: a real home-cooked meal.

After that, Dwaina was hooked on helping the homeless. To subsidize the cost of the food, she and her family sought help and donations from bakeries and grocery stores. Then, nearly every Friday night for an entire year, Dwaina, her mother, and her sisters made about one hundred meals for the shelter in Dallas. But Dwaina wanted to make more meals. The only way to do this, however, was to get more help, so Dwaina talked to her class at school. She told her classmates what her mother and sisters had been doing over the past year.

The following Friday, twenty-three kids from Dwaina's class came over to her house, each with some type of food to contribute. By midnight they'd prepared more than three hundred meals, enough for everyone in the shelter to have one.

Dwaina Brooks, now fourteen, has organized thousands of meals for the homeless in Dallas. She hopes to become a doctor and open her own clinic someday, but she thinks it's crazy to wait until then to start caring for others.

"Each of us should have some kind of concern in our hearts for other people," Dwaina says. "And we owe it, too. There isn't a one of us who hasn't been helped by someone else. You should always be ready to give back what people have given to you."

ANDREW BURNS

LEAVE YOUR BANKING TO HIM

When Andrew Burns goes to the bank in his hometown, he walks past the tellers, past the guards, and into his own office. Eleven years old, Andrew is the president of the Children's Bank in Omaha, Nebraska.

It all started in 1991, when Andrew's father was about to open the Enterprise Bank. Since his father owned the new bank, Andrew spent a lot of time there before it opened, cleaning up and doing odd jobs. Andrew got the idea that if he was good enough to be a janitor, then maybe he could do something more.

> **"If you want something bad enough you'll probably get it, so go for it right away, and don't wait."**

"During the construction I was cleaning up and getting paid," he said. "Once the bank opened I had nothing to do and I was bored. I got to thinking about what things the bank needed and what I could give it."

Andrew realized that the only thing the new bank didn't have was a special place just for kids. What the bank needed most was a branch for kids, so they would have someone their own age who could teach them about banking, money, and responsibility. Also, Andrew felt it would be more fun for kids to have a place of their own in the bank, and maybe this would make them more interested in saving money.

17

When he was eight years old, Andrew applied for a job at his father's bank—not just any job, but as the president of the Children's Bank. At first no one at the bank took his idea seriously, but Andrew wouldn't let up. He knew it was a good idea, because whenever he went to the bank with his parents, he saw only adults around and felt intimidated. Andrew talked about it a lot to his father and other bank employees, and explained how he felt as a kid in an "adult's bank." Finally they realized that it was a great idea, and the Children's Bank was born, becoming a permanent division of his father's Enterprise Bank.

Just as in a regular bank, youngsters come to the Children's Bank to open savings accounts and to get their questions answered about money, interest rates, and how a bank works. The only difference is that they are greeted and helped by a smaller-than-usual-size bank president.

For three days a week during the summer, and by appointment during the school year, hundreds of kids come to see Andrew at the bank. Sometimes Andrew has an assistant, but usually he's a one-man operation. There are more than 600 accounts in his bank, including one belonging to a one-year-old.

"I try to make the best use of the kids' money and put it to good use inside the bank," he says. "I'm a kid. I understand banking, and I understand their needs."

TAKE ACTION!

You're never too young to learn about money. Go to your local bank, or ask your parents and friends for a bank they recommend, and find out all you can. Maybe open a savings account and save for something you really want. If the banking bug bites you, why not find out if a bank in your area needs a children's branch of its own!

Andrew's success has inspired banks in Texas and New York to open children's branches.

"If you want something bad enough you'll probably get it," says Andrew, "so go for it right away, and don't wait."

During his free time, Andrew loves to play soccer, baseball, and the clarinet. He also likes to hang out with his friends, many of whom he met at the bank.

But when Andrew heads off to work, he leaves his sneakers at home. He changes out of his play clothes and puts on a dress shirt and a tie. After all, he *does* have a bank to run!

TOMMY CALDWELL
FOR THE LOVE OF CLIMBING

You might say that Tommy Caldwell knows the ropes. Tommy lives in Estes Park, Colorado, and he's been climbing mountains since he was four years old. His father, a mountain-climbing guide, taught Tommy everything he knows.

Tommy's climbs have taken him atop some of the highest mountains in the world, but his most celebrated climb wasn't far from home. Just before his thirteenth birthday, Tommy climbed the sheer east wall of Longs Peak, becoming the youngest person to climb this 14,256-foot-high summit, the highest in Rocky Mountain National Park in Boulder, Colorado.

Tommy and his father set off on their climb at two thirty in the morning, in total darkness. They left so early because Longs Peak is known for its afternoon rain and lightning storms—something climbers want to avoid at all costs. Wearing helmets, toting lots of granola bars and water, and carrying almost ten pounds of gear apiece, they began their ascent. The route Tommy and his dad took was ranked 5.10, representing a climb of severe difficulty. The most difficult climb in the world ranks 5.14.

To get to the rock wall, Tommy and his father had to first cross a glacier, and then trudge through deep snow. Once at the forbidding wall of stone, the two tied themselves together and took turns climbing. While one rested and held an anchored rope, the other ascended. As they approached the top of the peak, they had to dodge large chunks of ice that were beginning to fall from above. Tommy watched as the ice tumbled down the side of the mountain and landed hundreds of feet below. "The clouds were moving in, and it was getting really cold," says Tommy. "Seeing how long it took the ice to fall toward the earth below gave me an idea of how high I was."

TAKE ACTION!

Write down things you want to accomplish, and post them somewhere you can see them every day. Whether it's climbing a mountain or just doing better in a subject at school, the rewards are even greater when you set your own goals and then achieve them.

Near the top of the peak hail began to fall, and lightning streaked the sky. But the hardest obstacle was yet to come. An overhanging bulge, a part of the rock that extends out beyond the rest of the mountain wall, stood in their way. Tommy fit his fingers and feet into minute cracks in the rock and pulled himself onto the top of Longs Peak! The entire climb, up and back, took just under sixteen hours.

Besides the thrill that rock climbing gives Tommy, the sport allows him to spend time with his father. It also makes him feel good about himself. "Climbing really helps my self-esteem," Tommy says. "Even my grades are getting better."

Tommy keeps in shape by running, skiing, and using an artificial climbing wall that he keeps in the garage at home. And although he has already climbed some of the highest mountains in the world, he has set his sights on at least one more. "I want to do Everest," he says, ". . . and I will."

RACHEL CARTER
A FLIGHT FIT FOR A KID

Look, up in the sky! It's a bird. It's a plane. It's nine-year-old Rachel Carter, piloting her first trip across the country, in a single-engine plane. Rachel was the youngest female pilot ever to make a transcontinental trip from California to New York and back.

Since she was three years old Rachel has been around airplanes. Her father, Jimmy Carter (not the former U.S. president), is a flight instructor, and Rachel used to go to flight school with him and watch as he flew test flights and ran emergency procedures. When her father was at the controls, Rachel always rode in the back seat of the plane. In 1991, when Rachel's father flew from California to Tennessee, his six-year-old daughter also wanted to fly the plane. So Rachel's father let her sit on his lap. She put her hands on his as he held the controls and handled the plane.

"I was smiling so much my face hurt!"

From then on, Rachel wanted to fly somewhere no other girl her age had flown. She decided to make the trip across the country and back. "It became my dream," she says.

Three years later, with many flying lessons under her belt, Rachel and her father took off from San Diego, California. This time her father was in the back seat and Rachel was in charge. Together, they flew in a Piper Aero 3, a single-engine plane. Rachel had to sit on thick books and three pillows so she could reach the pedals.

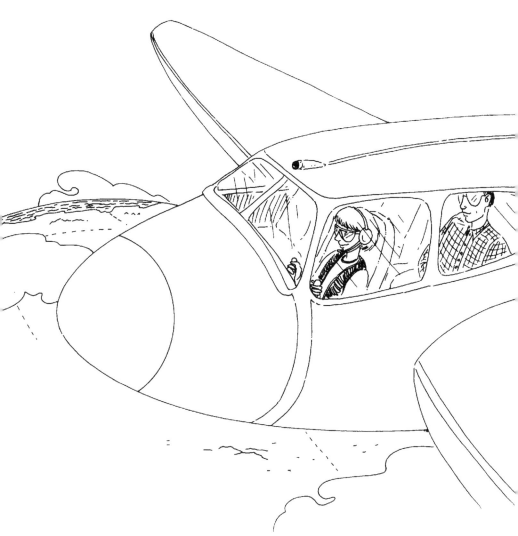

Their first stop was Albuquerque, New Mexico, which ended up being the toughest leg of the entire trip. "It was so bumpy, and the turbulence was the worst I've ever experienced," said Rachel.

The flight took her to places she had never been, such as Arkansas, where "the houses are so beautiful and so old." Before her trip she had never traveled farther east than Tennessee, where her grandmother lives.

Rachel landed in New York on March 24, three days after she'd left California. She arrived to enthusiastic cheers from the many people who met her at the airport. There were also television news cameras and photographers recording her historic flight. "It felt so good when I landed in New York," says Rachel. "I was smiling so much my face hurt!"

Rachel's father thinks she is a natural pilot and a quick study. "With the United States as her classroom, she's learned so much from this trip," her father said.

"Flying is pretty easy," says Rachel. "The hardest thing is having to wait for good weather." Fortunately, Rachel didn't have to contend with poor weather, and she arrived back in California on March 31, having completed her dream flight without a single problem . . . almost. Over Phoenix, Arizona, a huge 757 jet (about the size of five school buses lined up end to end) came uncomfortably close to the Carters' small plane. But they radioed the radar tower, the 757 shifted its course, and everything was fine.

Rachel especially loves flying at night because "it's so beautiful." When she grows up she wants to fly jets— F-14s—for the Blue Angels, the pilots who fly in air shows. In the meantime, Rachel has many more flights ahead of her and probably even greater adventures.

TAKE ACTION!

Okay, so you may not be ready to hop in a plane and fly to destinations unknown, but how about going somewhere you've never been, such as an art museum, an arboretum, or even your town's city hall? New experiences help you to shape your thoughts and opinions on things, and they may give you a little insight on which unknown places to explore next!

NICHOLE CONNOLLY

WHAT'S IN THE WATER?

What *lead* Nichole Connolly to put together a science project worthy of national recognition? Nichole found lead-contaminated water in an elementary school drinking fountain in her hometown of Statesville, North Carolina.

Science has always fascinated Nichole. It was while doing research for another project that Nichole first read about lead contamination—and the subject just wouldn't leave her mind. When the time came for her next science project, Nichole knew exactly what she wanted to explore. She decided to look into the safety of the water in the seven public schools in her district. Nichole, thirteen, had been doing science projects since she was in the third grade, but this project—"Schools . . . Water . . . Lead . . . Is There a Problem?"—is by far her most important work.

Nichole went around to the seven schools and, with the permission of each principal, took water samples from all of the drinking fountains and faucets in each one. She then contacted the Environmental Protection Agency (EPA), which recommended a private lab to test the water. After three months of gathering samples, working in the lab, and tracking results, Nichole discovered a problem.

The EPA rates 15.0 parts per billion (ppb) of lead as an acceptable limit in drinking water. Six of the seven school samples came back from the lab well under that level, most

> **"Science is a field of endless possibilities."**

ranging from 3.0 to 5.8 ppb, except for Pressly Elementary School. A drinking fountain in the main hallway of Pressly Elementary tested at 17.7 ppb, an unacceptably high amount, and much higher than any of the other six water samples.

Nichole's findings received national attention and helped her to win first place in the county science fair and an award from the Duke Power Energy Exploratorium in Cornelius, North Carolina, for achievement in environmental education. But most important, Nichole's project got officials in Statesville moving. Specialists were brought in to check Nichole's results (which were found to be accurate) and then to address the problem.

"The same day of the science fair the school system tested all of the water supplies [water pipes and drinking water], tested the contaminated supply, and replaced all of the piping and faucets," says Nichole. "Now it's safe.

"Science is a field of endless possibilities," says Nichole. "There are always new and challenging things to learn, and puzzles to solve."

Nichole's natural curiosity prompted her to question the safety of the schools' water. But it was her initiative and concern that caused her to carry out the experiments.

"Because of my project, people are starting to really think about whether the water is safe in their areas or schools," says Nichole. School systems across the country now routinely test their water supply for pollutants.

Nichole is pleased with the attention she has received, and hopes it helps girls realize that they can succeed in science, just as boys can. She's already decided that science is going to be a big part of her life. She plans to study medicine—possibly nuclear medicine—and become a doctor.

26

CHARO DARWIN

FOOD FROM THE 'HOOD

In April 1992, Los Angeles went to war, and hundreds of people were involved. It was the worst rioting in the city's history, and its effects still linger today. Charo Darwin lives in South-Central Los Angeles, one of the hardest-hit areas of the riots, and a place that is known for being dangerous and sometimes violent.

After the riots, Charo, fourteen, and her fellow students at Crenshaw High School decided they wanted to do something to help their devastated community. They got together and thought about what was needed, and what they could do to change people's attitudes about the neighborhood.

> "A lot of people think we're a joke, but we're doing something really positive."

One afternoon, Charo was gazing at the plot of land behind one of her classrooms. The shabby, quarter-acre lot struck her as a symbol of neglect, of something growing out of control. And suddenly it hit her. Maybe this school-owned lot could be the start of something truly special. Charo talked with her classmates and, after brainstorming different projects, decided it would be a great idea to plant a garden. The class asked their biology teacher if they could clean up the lot and use the land for some good. The teacher said yes, and she even added an incentive. If the kids would work on the garden on Saturdays, they'd get extra credit for

27

showing up and helping.

So Charo and thirty-nine other students began creating their garden. Over several Saturdays, the group labored together to clean up the garbage, pull out the weeds, prepare the soil, and plant seeds in the land they now claim as their own.

They grew several varieties of herbs and almost every kind of vegetable—from broccoli and cauliflower to snow peas and carrots—and gave much of the produce to needy people in their community. Soon everyone in the neighborhood knew about the garden, and many people came by on Saturdays to lend a hand to the group. Local companies began contributing seeds and materials.

About a year later, on one of their regular Saturday workdays, Charo and her friends decided that they wanted more out of their garden. Although it was a big success and they were even making a little money selling produce to the local farmer's market, they had bigger ideas. "We all realized that what we needed was to make more money," said Charo. "We needed money for tools and supplies for the garden, and for college. We came up with the idea to develop [and market] a salad dressing."

And so Food from the 'Hood, a natural food products company, was born at Crenshaw High School. The forty kids who worked the garden became student-owners and ran the business, down to the very last detail. They even designed the logo that would appear on the dressing bottles. They realized that the best thing they could do for their community was to get an education, so they decided that the company's profits would fund college scholarships for all the participants.

Their next step was to find a company to develop the recipe for their "Straight Out 'the Garden" all-natural creamy Italian dressing. They contacted a local salad dressing manufacturer and, after rejecting five different recipes, found a winner: a dressing that used fresh parsley and basil grown in their own garden.

Next they went to a food broker, a person who helps distribute food products. To the group's delight, all of the major grocery stores in Los Angeles bought their salad dressing. With "Straight Out 'the Garden" selling for $2.59 a bottle, Food from the 'Hood expected to make $100,000 by the end of 1994.

"This has been a real learning experience for all of us," says Charo. "A lot of people think we're a joke, but we're doing something really positive. Food from the 'Hood is like one big family . . . one big family business."

Not only are Charo and the other student-owners planting seeds in their garden, they're planting seeds of hope and growth in their community. Although it's a lot of work, and takes a lot of time and dedication, Charo feels that there's something very special about a garden. "You put something in the ground, water it, care for it, and it grows," says Charo.

CASEY GOLDEN

INVENTING TO A TEE

Casey Golden stepped onto his first golf course when he was five years old. He loved everything about golf, especially collecting the colorful golf tees. Little did he realize then that those small wooden tees would change the course of his life.

> **"The most challenging part is to realize that nothing happens overnight. It can take a long time and a lot of work."**

Five years later, Casey, then ten, noticed that many golfers just discarded their wooden golf tees once they broke, leaving them behind on the courses. Not only did they spoil the golfers' view, but Casey learned from the course greenskeepers that the tees damaged the blades and tires of the golf course lawn mowers. Why would people make golf tees out of a material that caused so many problems? Wasn't there a better way?

When Casey joined an afterschool course in creative analysis, all the students were asked to identify a problem and find a solution. Casey had the perfect problem to work on. Why not invent a tee that was biodegradable? (*Biodegradable* means "able to decay and become absorbed by the environment.") After thinking about it for some time, Casey did just that. He came up with the idea for "BIOtees," and the biodegradable golf tee was born.

First, Casey needed to invent a tee that would dissolve

with water, since golf courses are watered daily. His first recipe was very simple. He mixed flour and water, formed the mixture into a tee shape, and cooked it. The mixture did dissolve with water, but it took a long time and left a white, chalky residue.

Next, Casey tried mixing peat moss, grass seed, fertilizer, applesauce, and a special paste that dissolved when wet. The applesauce was suggested by a friend who discovered that it acted as a cement when cooked. Casey packed the mixture into a hollow Chap Stick tube, hardened it in the microwave, and carved it into a tee shape.

It worked! Casey's invention, which was entered by him and his science teacher, won grand prize in the 1989 Invent America! contest, a national school competition for students with unique inventions. Still not completely satisfied with the ingredients of his golf tee, Casey wrote to golf course greenskeepers around the country, asking for suggestions to improve his design. He learned that the fertilizer and grass seed in his prototype tees could damage some golf courses, since different courses use different kinds of grass. Casey removed the fertilizer and grass seed and replaced them with recycled

paper fiber and food by-products, all coated with a water-soluble film instead of applesauce. Once this film was broken down by water, moisture in the ground changed the tee into a loose mass in about twenty-four hours, causing no harm to the grass.

"The most challenging part is to realize that nothing happens overnight," he says. "It can take a long time and a lot of work."

Casey's family has since formed a company to manufacture BIOtees. So far they have orders for six million tees. If the company continues to sell that number each year, almost 3,400 trees could be saved every month.

In addition to running his growing business and being a member of the varsity golf team, Casey works hard in school. He dreams of becoming either a professional golfer or an environmental architect. One thing is for sure—either way, Casey plans on spending a lot of time on the golf course, using BIOtees!

KAREN GOMYO
ROOM FOR A VIOLIN

If Karen Gomyo lived in a mansion, she probably would never have learned to play the violin. As a small child, Karen's favorite instrument was the piano. So naturally, when Karen's mother encouraged six-year-old Karen to pick a musical instrument to learn, she chose the piano. The Gomyo family, however, didn't have the room for a piano in their small home in Montreal, Canada. The violin, they all agreed, was the next best choice.

Holding a child-sized violin under her chin, Karen started her first music lessons in school. The class was taught using the Suzuki method—a technique for teaching music to children at a very young age. In Suzuki classes, recorded music is played over and over, and children learn to play it by ear. Karen discovered she really liked playing the violin. But she was growing impatient. She wanted to play more difficult pieces. "I wanted to learn quickly, so I would practice every day, even if it was for only five minutes," says Karen. Soon she began practicing for longer periods of time and taking private lessons. She improved dramatically. Two years later, by the time she was eight, it was clear that Karen had a gift—a very special gift.

"Many people told me I was talented," says Karen, "but I didn't think so. I just enjoyed playing."

Before she was ten years old, Karen had played her violin throughout Canada.

She'd won many competitions, including first place in the Canadian Competition, the largest children's classical music competition in Canada. But the performance that was to most change her life took place when Karen was still only nine years old. She was performing a solo during an appearance with the Quebec Symphony Orchestra when Dorothy DeLay, a very special violin teacher from the Juilliard School in New York City, heard her play.

> "Many people told me I was talented, but I didn't think so. I just enjoyed playing."

"Ms. DeLay liked my playing very much and told me that she would be my teacher," said Karen. At seventy-seven years old, Ms. DeLay had taught many famous violinists at Juilliard, including Itzhak Perlman, Midori, and thirteen-year-old Sarah Chang, recognized as one of the best young violinists in the world.

Karen's parents made a great sacrifice for her. While Karen's father remained in Canada so he could keep his job to pay for Karen's music lessons, Karen and her mother moved to New York City so that Karen could begin studying at Juilliard.

"She is very kind, and a different kind of teacher," says Karen about Ms. DeLay. "She asks me how I feel about a piece and what images I see when I play."

During the week, Karen goes to the Professional Children's School, where she studies regular school subjects. Then, every day after school, she practices for four hours—for one hour after she has a snack, then for another three after dinner. On Saturdays Karen studies at Juilliard with Ms. DeLay. After her Saturday class, Karen rests, watches movies, or spends time with her friends. By Sunday she's back to her violin and her practicing.

"My teacher says I play differently than other people," says Karen. "It's like I have my own ideas and interpretation." Karen especially enjoys playing with an orchestra because, she says, "It feels like I'm lost in a world of music."

Karen's life is full of music, and that's the way she likes it. Whenever she can, Karen goes to violin concerts with her friends and her mom. She's even beginning to learn the piano. Karen plans to continue studying at Juilliard as long as she can, possibly through college. She takes her playing very seriously. "I love being a musician and wouldn't mind being really famous someday," she says.

Karen believes that it's important for every kid to know something that other kids don't know much about. "It's important to know something else, something different," she says. "It's important to experience different worlds."

Karen has experienced a lot on this planet, but the world she loves most is the world of music.

TAKE ACTION!

Have you ever thought about playing a musical instrument? Before you settle on one, try a few different instruments and listen to a variety of music. As you decide which you'd like to play, here are some important questions to discuss with your parents:

• Why do I want to play an instrument?
• Do I have time to practice?
• How much do lessons cost?
• How much does it cost to buy or rent the instrument?

AJA HENDERSON

IT'S ALL IN THE BOOKS

Ever since Aja Henderson was a little girl, she has loved books. Even before she could read, she would "play reading" by looking at the pictures in books and pretending to read the text to her stuffed animals.

Now she runs her own library.

"Ever since I was very, very small I read a lot," said Aja. "I'd go places in my books, and 'bored' was never in my vocabulary."

The only gifts Aja ever wanted for her birthday or other holidays were books. When she began receiving an allowance, she spent it on books. Little by little, Aja's book collection grew to more than 1,000 titles.

Kept in her family's den, Aja's vast collection filled several bookcases. There were books of fairy tales, adventure stories, biographies, books about families and friendships, and books about animals.

Aja's Baton Rouge, Louisiana, neighborhood was many miles from the public library. Since books were so important to her and had taught her so much about the world, Aja worried that the neighborhood kids were missing out by living so far from their public library. So she had an

"It's great to win an award for service projects, but the real award is the satisfaction you can get from helping others."

idea. Fourteen-year-old Aja invited the neighborhood kids to come to her house and borrow her books. And come they did! Kids arrived from all over, and were welcome anytime. Besides lending books, sometimes Aja read to the kids, and sometimes they read to her. She also tutored those kids who needed help with their reading.

Some days Aja had more than ten kids at her house at the same time—spread out on the floor, sitting on her lap, sharing chairs, all with books in their hands. Not only were they reading together, they were learning together. Aja had become their teacher and their friend.

"I was a support system for these kids," says Aja. "I'd read to them and help them with their homework, and show them the importance of knowing how to read."

Aja lent out her own books, the way a real library does. She had her own card catalog system and kept track of who borrowed which books and when they were due back. This taught the kids responsibility, and made them feel that they were trusted. Because of that trust, all of Aja's books were returned, and most of them on time.

In 1992, Aja was honored as a Presidential Point of Light for community service. She met President Bush at the awards ceremony and even had a Secret Service escort for the event. She also won the Clairol Sea Breeze Award, which recognized her spirit of public service.

"It's great to win an award for service projects, but the real reward is the satisfaction you can get from helping others," says Aja. "Just seeing kids develop a love for reading is thanks enough."

TAKE ACTION!

Think of something you're good at—such as reading, playing the piano, or swinging a baseball bat—and offer to tutor someone who could use your help. Sharing what you have already learned is often the most rewarding part of teaching.

Since receiving the presidential award, Aja has founded the Bookworm Network, an organization that works to promote reading and sharing of books throughout the country. "My parents taught me that if I saw a need and thought I could do something about it, to just try and take the initiative."

ANDREW HOLLEMAN
MORE THAN A FOREST

Twelve-year-old Andrew Holleman fought for almost a year to keep the forest he loved in his hometown of Chelmsford, Massachusetts, from being turned into a condominium complex. Also in jeopardy were nearby wetlands—the swampy home to at least three endangered species and the source of his hometown's water supply. To save the forest and the wetlands from being destroyed, Andrew knew he had to get smart— and get help, fast.

Andrew's fight for the land began when his mother showed him a letter she had received from a land developer. The letter explained how the woods across from their home were to be leveled in preparation for building new condominiums. Andrew had played in and explored that land since he was a young boy. In the summer he'd fish for bass in

the large stream that ran through the woods; in the winter he'd play hockey on the frozen water. All year long he'd spend hours there, whittling and thinking. He even went there when he got in trouble and needed a place to hide from his parents. It was unbearable for Andrew to think that the woods would soon be gone forever.

"I challenge kids to protect the earth. "

Andrew headed to the library to track down some information. His parents, who had already done a bit of research on the subject themselves, told him about the Hatch Act, a law that controlled the development of wetlands in Massachusetts. Many hours and several books later, Andrew found the information he needed. The Hatch Act stated that it was illegal to build without a permit within 100 feet of a wetland. Andrew figured that the developer, as well as a good portion of the community, didn't know about this act, so he took it upon himself to get the word out.

With an important town meeting just four weeks away, Andrew had only a month to spread the news. He decided to write a petition opposing the development and ask voters in the area to sign it. He also created a petition at school and, even though he and his classmates couldn't vote, he hoped that their opinion would still be considered important.

Next, he contacted the state's Audubon Society Environmental Health Line to find out which animals make their home in the wetlands. Three endangered species lived on the land: the wood turtle, the yellow salamander, and the great blue heron.

With 180 signatures in hand, Andrew and his parents went to the meeting. More than 250 people showed up, mostly because of Andrew's tireless efforts to make sure the community was informed. Andrew felt calm and confident, feelings that come only with being prepared. He had spent a solid month organizing and writing down his thoughts. The heartfelt speech he delivered at the meeting was met with thunderous applause.

"I tried to keep my cool," says Andrew. "When I spoke I just said what was on my mind, and was very respectful."

But the fight wasn't over. The developer wouldn't back down. For ten more months the debate raged on. Meetings were held with the conservation commission, the zoning board, and the appeals board to decide whether the condominiums could be built. Andrew went to every meeting. He kept up hope that his hard work, and people's growing awareness, would ultimately save the land.

Finally, victory arrived. A soil test at the site revealed that sewage from the proposed condominiums would indeed pollute the town water supply. The fight was over.

Although it was a lot of work, Andrew knew it was well worth the effort. "Something had to be done," says Andrew. "I did this because of my love for the environment and because if I didn't, probably no one would have.

"I challenge kids to protect the earth," says Andrew. They are, after all, going to be around a lot longer than adults, and Andrew feels it's up to them to fight for the future.

TAKE ACTION!

The smartest way to fight for something you believe in is to arm yourself with information. One of the best places to get information is your public library, where you'll find newspapers, magazines, and city records. Inform yourself, and don't be afraid to share what you've learned with other people.

GINA JALBERT

A STAR OF TENNIS

Gina Jalbert, of Arcadia, California, is a champion. Born with spina bifida, a condition that eventually causes paralysis from the waist down, Gina must use a wheelchair to get around.

But that hasn't stopped Gina from winning four Junior National Wheelchair Tennis championships. Her first win took place when she was eleven years old, making her the youngest person ever to win the competition. If that isn't enough, based on past championships and overall tournament wins, Gina is also ranked the number-one junior player in the United States.

Before Gina turned nine years old, she was able to get around with leg braces. But by the time she was ten her condition had worsened. She had her first major surgery, to explore whether anything could be done to prevent her spine from deteriorating further, but it was clear that she would now need a wheelchair. It was at this same time that Gina saw her first wheelchair tennis tournament. She was amazed at how fast wheelchair athletes could get around, and she instantly knew that *that* was what she wanted to do too.

> "If you have something that you really love . . . do it to its fullest, and don't let anything stop you."

Gina started playing wheelchair tennis soon after, and she has been playing ever since. In the past six years, Gina, now seventeen, has won thousands of tournaments and matches, many of them against boys. She likes the challenge. "Boys hit hard—they don't give girls a chance," Gina says. "But for me, playing boys is just another challenge."

The rules for wheelchair tennis are the same as for regular tennis, except the players are allowed two bounces before the ball must be hit. Also, a player can win a point if he or she hits the opponent's wheelchair with a ball.

Gina plays tennis almost every day and has two coaches, one who uses a wheelchair and one who does not.

TAKE ACTION!

If you are physically challenged, don't let that stop you from trying something you've always wanted to do. Or if you know someone with a physical disability, find out what activity they'd like to try, then do it with them. Try and think up new ways to play games or sports that could include someone with special obstacles.

Every season Gina sets new goals for herself, such as winning specific tournaments and playing other sports, and so far, almost every year she has attained them. "If you have something that you really love . . . do it to its fullest, and don't let anything stop you," Gina says. Her love for tennis and other sports keeps her motivated and her spirits up. Gina also competes in other wheelchair sports, including basketball, weightlifting, racing, skiing, and badminton.

Sports have given Gina the opportunity to travel, made her more outgoing and confident, and allowed her to meet many very special people.

"Most people don't know about wheelchair sports," she says. That is why Gina serves as an adviser for videos and movies that help educate people about wheelchair sports. Since she was fourteen, Gina's work has focused on promoting wheelchair sports and on making the public aware that people with disabilities can compete in sports on a professional level.

"Sports have opened my eyes toward attitudes about disabled people and made me want to do more and get more accomplished in my life," says Gina.

KORY JOHNSON
CHILDREN FOR A SAFE ENVIRONMENT

In 1989, Kory Johnson's sixteen-year-old sister, Amy, died from heart disease. Her death was caused by contaminated tap water that Kory's unsuspecting mother drank while she was pregnant with Amy. To help ease their pain, eleven-year-old Kory and her mom joined a bereavement group, a support group for people who have suffered the loss of a loved one.

Kory and her mother met other people in the group who had also lost family members because of the contaminated water. They discovered that they lived in something called a "cancer cluster"—an area where people are at least twice as likely to get cancer than in other places in the United States. As soon as Kory learned about this, she could no longer stand around and do nothing. She couldn't believe that other kids around her were also dying because of the poisoning of the environment. Her time had come to get involved, so in 1990, less than a year after her sister's death, she founded Children for a Safe Environment, a group of youth activists concerned with environmental health.

Today Kory's organization has more than 350 members throughout her home state of Arizona. "When I started, I

> "If there's something that you believe in or something that you want to get involved with, don't ever give up."

didn't even know what a protest was," says Kory. Today, not only does she know about protests, she's participated in many.

"Some people don't understand why I'm giving so much of my time to the environment," said Kory. "I've learned to become a fighter and to question authority. Now that I'm educated and know the truth about our environment, I have something to say."

As the founder and president of Children for a Safe Environment, Kory goes to local schools and talks to younger kids about recycling and the environment, and how they have to learn to protect it today so that there may be a safe and healthy world when they have their own children.

With older kids and adults she talks about environmental racism, which is the polluting of poor neighborhoods where there is a large minority population, as well as the hiring of minority workers to do jobs under unsafe conditions, such as working with sewage and toxic waste.

"I've seen so many people with different issues and stories," says Kory. "Working on the environment has changed me and taught me to stick up for what I believe in."

Kory says her mom is her hero and role model. Together they have become two of the most respected environmental activists in Arizona.

To stop an incinerator from burning hazardous waste near her hometown, Kory wrote letters of protest to the governor, local newspapers, health departments, and the Department of Environmental Quality. She mailed fliers to residents and helped organize a candlelight rally at the state's capitol. For three hours, hundreds of children from all over the state went to the microphone one by one and spoke about protecting the environment.

"My main focus right now is educating kids," says Kory. "A lot of adults have started to listen to kids, so our voice is important."

Kory has been awarded the Environmental Protection Agency Award and the first-ever John Denver Windstar Environmental Youth Award for her tireless crusade for the environment. She has also been chosen as a "Giraffe" by the Giraffe Project, an organization that honors youth activists all over the country for their dedication and work.

Sometimes Kory doesn't feel like going out and talking to people, making speeches, or teaching younger kids what she knows, but she pushes herself to do it anyway because she always learns something.

"Don't ever give up," says Kory. "If there's something that you believe in or something that you want to get involved with, don't ever give up. It will always be worth it if you believe in it that strongly."

TAKE ACTION!

Find out what's happening in your area and volunteer for a cause that interests you. Most organizations not only welcome kids, they encourage their participation. To find out more about Children for a Safe Environment, write to:

Children for a Safe Environment
Attn: Kory Johnson
517 East Roanoke #A
Phoenix, AZ 85004

JUSTIN LEBO

FROM JUNK TO JOY

At a garage sale, ten-year-old Justin Lebo of Saddle Brook, New Jersey, found an old rundown bicycle in need of a home. Justin's hobby was bike racing, and although he already had two racing bikes of his own, he knew this old junker had possibilities. For six dollars and fifty cents, Justin bought it and took it home.

> "A bike is like a book. It opens up a whole new world."

Everything on the bicycle was broken—the grips, the pedals, the brakes, the seat, the spokes— but Justin knew he could fix it up. He'd become very good at fixing bikes while working with his father, who shared his passion for bike racing. The family garage was already set up like a bike shop, with bicycle frames and tires hanging from hooks on the ceiling, and tools everywhere. In no time the bike was riding well and looked brand-new. A week later Justin bought another old, junky bike and soon it, too, was ready for the road.

But something about the two bikes sitting in the garage began to eat at Justin. The thing he loved about old bikes wasn't riding them, but the challenge of making something new and useful out of something broken and neglected. And then suddenly Justin had an idea. Why not give the bikes to kids who couldn't afford one?

When Justin was younger, his family had lived near the Kilbarchan Home for Boys in Paterson, New Jersey. Justin called the director of the home and asked whether the boys there would like the two refurbished bikes. The youngsters would love them, the director said. So Justin and his mother loaded the two-wheelers into the car and drove them right over. As soon as the bikes were taken out of the trunk, two boys ran out, jumped on the bikes, and pedaled away. Justin and his mother couldn't have been happier.

That was five years and 250 bikes ago. Until Justin was sixteen, he used much of his allowance and most of his spare time finding old bikes, fixing them up, and giving them away to those less fortunate.

But after an article about him appeared in a local paper, hundreds of people called and offered their old bicycles to him for free. "People would call me up and ask me to come over and pick up their old bicycles," he said. "Or I'd be working in the garage, and a car would drive up and the driver would leave a two-wheeler." Soon, so many bicycles were pouring in that Justin had to begin refusing them unless

they were the exact models he needed. People who didn't have bicycles to donate also began to give money to help pay for bike parts.

Many people have asked Justin why he spends so much time restoring bikes just to give them away. "All you'd have to see are the kids on the bikes to understand," he says. Their joy inspires him.

"Once I heard a kid who got one of my bikes say, 'A bike is like a book; it opens up a whole new world.' That's how I feel too. It made me happy to know that kid felt that way. That's why I do it."

Justin has given bicycles and tricycles to children in foster homes, in a home for children with AIDS, and in a battered-women's shelter, among many others. He continues to this day to give his time and heart to his community.

"When I was four or five years old, my mom taught me to share," says Justin. "That's how I was raised."

TAKE ACTION!

If you see something in the trash or at a yard sale that you think someone could use or enjoy, take it home, clean it up, and give it away. Go through your old toys and clothes for things you've outgrown, then donate them to a group whose cause you feel is worthwhile.

JAWAUNA MCMULLEN

FOR THE RUN OF IT

From the time she was five years old, the figure of Jawauna McMullen running alongside her older brother LaShaun was a familiar sight to the people who lived in their low-income housing district, Bedford-Stuyvesant, one of the toughest neighborhoods in Brooklyn, New York. But it was LaShaun who first noticed *how* Jawauna ran. And that was *fast*. She was faster than him!

Now seventeen, Jawauna is probably the most talented middle-distance runner in the United States. She's the best high school runner in the country in the seventeen-to-eighteen age division. And in 1993 alone, she won the Indoor and Outdoor National Scholastic Championships in the 800 meters, the USA Track and Field Junior Championships, and the Junior Pan Am Games in Canada. She's broken national records, too. Although Jawauna races several distances, her best is the half-mile.

"Winning isn't everything, but if I do run well there are rewards, and I get to go places."

Sometimes called One-Eye Joe by her friends because she is blind in her left eye, Jawauna has overcome more than just a physical handicap. As infants, she and her brother were abandoned by their parents. But they were lucky. An amazingly loving and supportive family, with eight kids of their own, adopted the two children. Jawauna's adop-

tive mother, Lena, is her best friend,
her hero, and one of her greatest fans.

Jawauna's running competitions have taken her all over
the country and to many parts of the world. She's seen and
experienced things she never even dreamed of. There was a
time, though, when Jawauna was fifteen, that she thought
about quitting track. She was uncomfortable with all the
attention being paid to her and found it difficult to concen-
trate in school. Tutoring helped, as did the encouragement
of her stepbrother Stephen. He taught Jawauna that if she
really worked hard, she could do anything—and do it well.

Jawauna trains every day for almost four hours. To get to
her track club, she must travel almost an hour each way by
subway and bus. Her coach, Carol Jones, is also her god-
mother.

"Jawauna finds a way to win," says her coach. "She loves
running and digs down deep inside and just does it. When

she gets on the track, her confidence is amazing, and she's learned to overcome her partial blindness."

Still, sometimes Jawauna's vision loss makes running—and winning—challenging. Jawauna has trouble seeing runners on her left, her blind side. To compensate, she accelerates quickly in front of the field. She knows that if she stays in the pack she might become visually confused and fall, or have trouble making a turn. Once she even ran into a shot put area next to the track when she became disoriented trying to get around the leader in a race.

But mostly Jawauna just wins . . . and wins . . . and wins. She is determined to do her best, and if she continues winning, she will most likely represent the United States in the 1996 Summer Olympics.

"Winning isn't everything," says Jawauna, "but if I do run well, there are rewards, and I get to go places. I think I like getting away just as much as winning."

Jawauna hopes to be a coach someday, to keep girls off the street and help them develop their own interests. Jawauna knows firsthand that being good at something does have its benefits.

In Jawauna's neighborhood, where drug dealers roam free, she is spared their harassment. "If the drug dealers see me coming, they put away their stuff," she says. "They do it because they have respect for me. I don't think they'd do it for anyone else—except maybe my mother."

CHARLIE MEIER
AN ARTIST WHOSE WORK FLOATS

Like many kids, Charlie Meier loves parades. As a young boy growing up in Pasadena, California, home of the famous Tournament of Roses Parade, Charlie dreamed of the day that his family would see the parade live, and not on TV. The parade was practically on his doorstep, but tickets to the spectacular event were almost impossible to get because they were in such high demand.

> **"Make somebody's day a little brighter, even if it's just for a few hours on New Year's Day."**

And then Charlie's dream came true. When he was ten years old, his family entered a drawing and won grandstand tickets to see the parade. Charlie was blown away by the experience. The Tournament of Roses is a particularly beautiful parade to watch up close, because every float is completely covered with different varieties of thousands and thousands of flowers. It was more amazing, more fantastic than he ever imagined.

Charlie was mesmerized and knew he had found something he wanted to try. He became fascinated with floats. To him, they were moving, three-dimensional pieces of art. Charlie read in the newspaper that most of the Tournament of Roses floats were built and decorated by volunteers. Charlie was ready to sign up, but the parade rules said individuals had to be at least sixteen years old to volunteer.

Charlie would have to wait six more years. He was crushed. There must be a way around this rule, he thought.

Charlie's mother knew that their city, South Pasadena, held a yearly design contest for its official float. She suggested to Charlie that he might think of an idea for a float and enter the competition. She knew it was a long shot, but Charlie was up for the challenge.

In 1989, when he was eleven years old, Charlie submitted a design for the 1990 parade. His idea came in third place. Charlie kept exploring and developing ideas, doing research on past floats, reading up on parades and designs, and preparing for the following years' competitions.

In 1991, Charlie designed a float called "Star Stuck," showing two aliens playing with a captured spaceship. Charlie is a real fan of science fiction and space. Out of the more than seventy ideas submitted, Charlie's concept for "Star Stuck" was chosen to represent South Pasadena in the 1992 parade. This made Charlie, at thirteen, the youngest float designer in the parade's 103-year history. "I think they liked it so much because it was a real fantasy," Charlie says.

Once his design was selected, Charlie had to finalize his original drawings and supervise flower selections for the float's decoration. He even got to ride in the flower-festooned spaceship as the astronaut! Charlie's float didn't win any special parade awards, but "nothing could take away from the incredible

TAKE ACTION!

Write to organizations for information about any unusual jobs that may appeal to you, such as making parade floats, being a ball girl, or becoming a clown. You won't know what you can do, or where your real talent lies, if you don't try.

excitement of the day," he remembers.

Two years and many designs later, Charlie had his second float design accepted. This idea centered around a ladybug and her family, which he called "First Outing." Since the general theme of the 1993 parade was fantastic adven-

tures, Charlie thought of the adventures that ladybugs must have, being so small and flying wherever they chose to go. The float was to be built in four parts, with the main float, the mother ladybug, thirty feet long, and the three smaller floats—representing the children—all connected to one another. "I've always liked representing things that are really small in real life on a very large scale," says Charlie. "And a ladybug seemed the perfect thing."

According to Charlie, the trickiest part about designing a float is being able to actually translate an idea into a three-dimensional object. To create "First Outing," Charlie had to bring together construction workers, welders, mechanics, and dozens of volunteers who would scramble together a few days before the parade applying the more than 30,000 flowers needed to cover the float. His ladybugs cost almost $50,000 to build, money that would all be donated from the city.

This time Charlie was responsible for all float decisions, including how the float would look, how fast it would move, where it would be built, what materials would be used, what types of flowers were to be selected, and what parts would be animated. The most difficult flowers to find were red carnations, because the parade takes place right after Christmas, and red flowers are in short supply during the holiday season.

After a year of meetings, and long hours of planning and finalizing designs and construction, New Year's Day came along. Charlie's float, with the help of more than seventy people, was ready to roll.

"It's really amazing," says Charlie. "You sit back and you're awestruck. I put so much of myself into it, and to watch it come out so amazingly beautiful is a thrill I can hardly describe."

Charlie's ladybug float won the Founders Trophy, an award given for the best overall float built and decorated by volunteers. And Charlie became the youngest person to win an award in the Tournament of Roses Parade.

"Building a float is a great way to unify the community and learn to work with many different people," says Charlie. Although a parade float has a short life, it doesn't matter to Charlie. It is worth it, he says, because he can "make somebody's day a little brighter, even if it's just for a few hours on New Year's Day."

Charlie has ideas for about 400 more floats, and certainly plans to make designing and building floats a big part of his future. "This is the most original, spectacular art form in the world today," says Charlie. "Being able to be part of that is just priceless to me."

CHRISTIAN MILLER

FOR THE SEA TURTLES

Very early in the morning, when most kids are fast asleep, sixteen-year-old Christian Miller of Palm Beach, Florida, is at the beach. But he's not surfing, swimming, or messing around; he's looking for sea turtles.

Sea turtles are reptiles that live in the ocean. The females come up on the beach to lay their eggs, which they bury in deep holes in the sand, and then they return to the ocean. When the turtle eggs hatch three months later, the baby hatchlings climb out of their nests and make a mad dash to the ocean. But sometimes the babies have trouble digging themselves out, and they die from the heat or the weight of the sand. Dogs, crabs, and other animals will also often find and eat them.

So every day at dawn, Christian patrols the beach, checking on turtle nests and digging out hatchlings that are trapped under the sand.

When Christian was eight, he and his family moved to Palm Beach, Florida, from their farm in Maryland. On the farm, Christian had been surrounded by many different animals. But in Palm Beach, Christian didn't see *any* wild animals except for an occasional tiny dead sea turtle on the beach behind his family's new home. Christian wanted to know how the turtles were

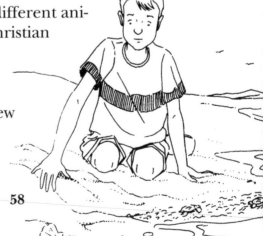

dying, and if there was anything he could do to help them.

Christian told the organizer of a local beach cleanup about his concern for the turtles, and was referred to the Florida Department of Natural Resources. He was then put in touch with a group of volunteers who were rescuing turtles. Christian learned that he needed a special permit to work with sea turtles, because they are an endangered species. It took him a year of training before he could be issued a permit from the Department of Natural Resources. During that time he learned all about sea turtles, the different species, their nests, how to handle them, and how to keep accurate records. Christian had to pass several tests administered by a Department representative, including how to locate a nest, how to know if a hatchling is in trouble, and how to teach people on the beach to be aware of turtle behavior.

To date, Christian has saved more than 17,000 baby sea turtles. Each day during the nesting season from May to October, Christian wakes up at six A.M., before the sand gets too hot, and patrols the three-mile stretch of beach behind his house for two to three hours. He searches the sand for tracks to the ocean made by baby turtles, then follows the tracks back to the nests. Christian marks the area surrounding each nest with brightly colored stakes that stay in place until the nest is empty, so people won't step on any hatchlings or eggs.

When he finds a hatched baby turtle that didn't escape with the others, he carries it to the water and lets it swim away.

Christian must keep careful records of his beach patrols. He writes down the number of turtles rescued from each nest and the number of hatched, unhatched, and fertilized eggs. There are four to six hundred nests on the beach that Christian patrols, and each nest holds an average of 110 eggs. Christian checks as many nests as he can, sometimes as many as a dozen a day. At the end of the season, he sends his data to the United States Department of Natural Resources, which uses the information as part of its ongoing research to help understand the declining sea turtle population.

Christian believes that his work with sea turtles has made him a more patient person. It has also made him more environmentally aware. "We can't all save sea turtles," he says, "but each of us can do a small part for the environment."

In 1993, Christian was the keynote speaker and representative for North America at the United Nations Environmental Program's Global Youth Forum in Colorado. In the speech he made to more than a thousand students from thirty-seven countries, Christian spoke of how important it is for people to get involved.

"One person can make a difference," Christian says. "I'm living proof of that."

TAKE ACTION!

Contact local or national organizations and offer your help. If you love animals, as Christian does, why not contact your local Audubon Society to find out about *their* animal rescue programs? Or contact your city's Humane Society and offer to feed, walk, or groom animals at a shelter. One person *can* make a difference. Your involvement and commitment will inspire others to join in. For more information about protecting endangered wildlife, write to:

World Wildlife Fund
Attn: Sheila Thomas, Public Information Dept. WWF
1250 24th Street, N.W.
Washington, D.C. 20037

MELISSA POE

KIDS FOR A CLEAN ENVIRONMENT

Like many kids, nine-year-old Melissa Poe likes to park herself, on occasion, in front of the tube. And why shouldn't she? It was while watching an episode of her favorite TV show, *Highway to Heaven*, that Melissa's life was dramatically changed. The program showed how polluted the world might become if people continue to disrespect the earth. Melissa was extremely moved by the message.

"I was scared I might die young because of it—that the world would be an ugly place to live. I worried that when I have kids, my kids might die young too," Melissa says.

> **"It's our future and it's our world, too."**

So Melissa wrote a letter to President Bush, asking him to help stop pollution. He didn't write back. Melissa figured that he didn't answer her letter because she was a kid, so she came up with another way to get his attention. While driving in the car with her mother, Melissa noticed a billboard and thought, what a great way to get a message across! If she got her letter printed on a billboard, then more people would see it, and maybe the president would *have to* listen to her.

With her mother's help, Melissa contacted an advertising company in her hometown of Nashville, Tennessee, and asked if it would print her letter on a billboard without charge. The company agreed to print the letter, but she would have to pay fifty dollars for the paper. To raise the money, Melissa had a yard sale. And that was only the beginning. Melissa was thinking big and decided she wanted her letter to appear on billboards all over the United States. With the help of the advertising company, who gave Melissa many national contacts, more than two hundred and fifty billboards were put up across the country, including one in Washington, D.C. Her letter on the billboard read:

Dear Mr. President,

I want to keep on living 'til I am 100 years old. . . . You and other people, maybe you could put up signs saying: Stop Pollution, It's killing the World. PLEASE help me stop pollution, Mr. President. Please, if you ignore this letter, soon we will die of pollution of the ozone layer.

Please help,
Melissa

Even though Melissa never heard from the president, the billboards got a lot of attention from newspapers and environmental supporters all across the country.

Melissa's classmates saw her billboards around, and they, too, wanted to get involved in the fight against pollution. So Melissa formed an organization of kids who cared about, and were willing to work at, protecting the environment.

Kids for a Clean Environment, Kids F.A.C.E., began in 1989 with only six people, including Melissa and her older brother. Today the group has more than 200,000 members, with 2,000 chapters throughout the world, including China, Greece, and Australia.

Kids F.A.C.E. publishes a newsletter that goes out to more than two million people. It reports on what people around the world are doing in their communities to help the environment, and includes projects that can be done at home. Sometimes people write letters and send drawings to Melissa, which she prints in the newsletter.

"I'm not surprised that so many kids got involved," said

Melissa. "It's our future and it's our world, too." As the CEO ("Child Executive Officer"), Melissa develops and runs projects for the organization. The group has formed the "Adopt a Manatee" program, which helps kids learn about this endangered species, and also a project called Children's Forest, which promotes learning about forests and the importance of trees to the environment.

Kids F.A.C.E. is also putting together a Kids Earth Flag, which will be made up of drawings of what the world looks like today and what kids want it to look like. Melissa hopes it will be the largest flag ever made by kids.

"Kids do pay attention," says Melissa. "They really notice things."

Likewise, people have been noticing Melissa. In 1992, she traveled to Rio de Janeiro, Brazil, as one of six children to speak at the global Earth Summit Forum's "Voices of the Future." She also attended the Youth World Council and a Washington, D.C., town meeting with Vice President Al Gore in 1993.

Running Kids F.A.C.E. is a lot of work, involving weekly meetings, public speaking, and organizing the efforts of kids, but Melissa knows how important it is. "I'm helping out," she says. "I only hope that what I'm doing right now teaches kids about what's going on in our environment and that we can make a difference in our future."

PATRICK REID
A DIFFERENT KIND OF SWIM

How would you like to share your favorite swimming spot with fish, seals, seagulls, and an occasional oil tanker? Thirteen-year-old Patrick Reid does. His swimming "spot" is the San Francisco Bay.

Patrick's father is a member of the South End Rowing Club, a private club that has a cove for swimming in the bay. When Patrick was five, his father first took him to the cove, and from then on the two of them made swimming a regular activity. The young boy loved to swim, and soon began challenging himself to swim longer and longer distances.

After preparing himself for quite some time, ten-year-old Patrick broke a thirty-five-year-old record by becoming the youngest person to swim from Alcatraz Island to San Francisco, a total of one and three-quarter miles. The water temperature on the day of his swim was sixty-two degrees, about twenty degrees colder than a normal heated pool. It took Patrick about an hour to swim the distance, but he never felt cold or scared. His father swam next to him and encouraged him all the way to a new record.

Soon Patrick was ready for his next challenge: the two-mile Golden Gate Bridge swim. Patrick entered the water and swam from one end of the bridge to the other and back. Amazed and distracted by the vastness of the bridge, Patrick swam a bit slower, hardly taking his eyes off the huge bridge above. He was eleven years old.

Trying to top his latest achievement, Patrick decided his next swim would be from the Bay Bridge to the Golden Gate Bridge, a distance of 5.9 miles. Aware that he could become the youngest person to complete this swim, and that a lot of people might be interested in what he was doing, he decided to use the public's interest for the good of others. Patrick had read in the newspaper about a nonprofit treatment center for emotionally disturbed children, and that was exactly the kind of group he wanted to help. He would swim to raise money for the center.

> "It's a lot more fun to use your talents for some good."

On July 3, 1992, at 5:40 A.M., while most of San Francisco was sleeping, Patrick and his swimming partner, his father, hit the cold bay waters. They left early to avoid the fog that can be expected to roll over the water anytime between late morning and mid-afternoon.

They scheduled the swim so that Patrick would be swimming in an ebb, or low, tide. The tide, which was heading out of the bay, helped to push the young swimmer along like a motor. For the first half-hour of the swim, Patrick swam both the freestyle and the breaststroke, conserving as much energy as possible for later in the swim.

"I like the challenge of swimming in rough water," he says, "but the water was so rough that day that sometimes I couldn't see where I was going."

One hour and thirteen minutes later, with family and friends cheering him on, Patrick became the youngest person to swim from the Bay Bridge to the Golden Gate Bridge, his longest swim ever. (Without the force of the ebb tide working with the young swimmer, the entire swim would have taken close to four hours.)

"The worst part of the swim is the first two minutes, because that is when you really feel the cold," says Patrick. "From that point on, your body is numb."

When Patrick climbed out of the water, he felt tired and a bit sick, but he was also very happy. Not only had he accomplished something he had set his sights on, but he had also raised $8,000 in pledges.

"It's a lot more fun to use your talents for some good," said Patrick. "It's important to help kids who aren't as lucky as I am."

After Patrick collected the pledges, he went to the children's treatment center and presented the check to the director. Among other things, the money bought new clothing and toys for the children. "When kids from the treatment center wrote me cards and told me I was their hero, that was the best thing," says Patrick.

Patrick's friends sometimes think he's crazy to swim in cold, rough waters, but "it's fun, it's unique, and not many people do it," says Patrick. "And if I can help other kids just by swimming, then I will keep on swimming."

MARIA SANSONE

FROM THE COURTS TO THE TUBE

Maria Sansone has an agent, a career, and a résumé that would make many adults envious. And she's twelve years old.

It all began in 1992 when Maria went to a basketball game with her grandparents. Maria, a basketball fanatic and the point guard for her school team in Erie, Pennsylvania, was chosen from the athletes in her area to be in a halftime slam-dunk contest for kids. She thrilled the crowd with spectacular dribbling and stunts, including hanging onto a specially lowered hoop rim after her dunk. Following the game, Maria was interviewed on WJET-TV, the local television station. The sports anchor from the station was impressed by Maria's easy way with words and her obvious knowledge of sports. And apparently, other people noticed as well. The newsroom received dozens of calls inquiring about Maria, wanting to know more about her.

Almost before she knew what had happened, Maria was asked to join the news team at WJET-TV as a sportscaster for kids. The next two years flew by as Maria learned the ropes of interviewing, television newscasting, and being comfortable in front of the camera. Today she hosts a weekly feature for the station called *Down to Size*, which focuses on student athletes, like herself, and professional sports figures. On her program Maria has interviewed dozens of kids as well as many famous sports figures such as Michael Jordan, Buffalo Bills quarterback Jim Kelly, and Pittsburgh Steelers coach Bill Cowher.

"Maria absolutely loves sports, and she just loves to talk," says her father, Tom. "She's a natural sportscaster."

In addition to her weekly series for WJET-TV, Maria was assigned by ABC Sports to cover the 1993 Little League World Series. Most recently, she has signed with ABC Sports to host *Wide World of Sports for Kids*. The first episode aired nationally in February 1994 and featured Maria interviewing kids training to become figure-skating champions. Other programs include young jockeys and their horses as well as Little League teams who make it into the championships.

Just like other celebrities, Maria has an agent who, along with her father, handles her publicity and business dealings. But Maria doesn't think of her work on television as "business." It's just something that she really enjoys. "I'm going to stick with broadcasting for a while," she says, "because I really like it."

It's obvious to Maria that many kids love sports. In every sports program she hosts, she tries to give youngsters a peer connection to sports, and express a kid's perspective.

When Maria's not at school or traveling across country on assignment, she can often be found at home watching the New York Knicks, her favorite team. She occasionally makes time for her second-favorite thing, playing the piano. But that's usually during the off-season only.

HEATHER STRANGE

A VERY SPECIAL CLOWN

Loveheart is like any other clown who loves to make people laugh. She dresses up in silly costumes and visits sick people and others who need to be cheered up. But Loveheart is different— she's only nine years old.

When Loveheart is not Loveheart, she is Heather Strange of Houston, Texas. Heather has a disability called cerebral palsy. Because of damage to her brain before she was born, Heather has trouble walking. By the time she was six, Heather could barely stand, and doctors said she might never walk again. In an effort to slow down the progression of her condition,

> **"You get to see the children smile. That's the best part."**

Heather had to spend six weeks in the hospital and have five separate surgeries on her right leg. It was there, at Shriners' Hospital for Crippled Children in Houston, Texas, that Heather met her first clown.

On Halloween night, medical students dressed as clowns came to visit her and the other children at the hospital. "They made me feel so good, and I saw how they cheered everybody up," said Heather. "The clowns were very color-ful, and full of smiles and funny tricks." Heather realized that she, too, wanted to make people feel good, especially if they were sick. She decided then that she would become a clown.

During her hospital stay, Heather thought constantly

about clowns. She read
books about clowns and
watched television shows that
featured clowns. She even
drew pictures of them to
make herself laugh!

A year later, after Heather
was healthy and feeling
much stronger at home, she
began pestering her parents
to send her to clown school.
Convinced by his daughter's
determination to be a clown,
Heather's father enrolled
her in the Cheerful Clown School in Missouri City, Texas.
And because he was so moved by the difference the clowns
had made to his daughter when she was feeling so down, he
enrolled himself in clown school too.

At first, the teachers at the school were not sure Heather
would take the program seriously. She was only seven years
old, much younger than the other students, and they were
afraid she would be there only to have fun. Her dedication
convinced them otherwise.

Clown school met on Saturdays for seven weeks. There,
she learned how to tell jokes and do tricks, how to make up
skits, and how to design costumes and makeup. After many
days of practice, and a lot of hard work, Heather became
the youngest person to graduate from the Cheerful Clown
School.

Heather knew where she wanted to perform after gradu-
ation. She returned to the hospital—to try and make the
children there feel the way she had felt when the clowns had
visited her.

"You get to see the children smile," says Heather. "That's

70

the best part."

When Heather performs, all of her worries go away. "It's like I'm in a different body when I'm performing. Like I'm a different person," she says. "My clown doesn't have disabilities. It makes me come into a world of niceness, not the other world."

Heather is right-handed, and because of her cerebral palsy she has limited use of her right arm. Putting on makeup is particularly hard. Sometimes she gets frustrated to the point of tears, but she just takes her time and asks for help from others—especially her father.

These days, Heather is walking much better. She is performing year-round, usually at the hospital but also at birthday parties, parades, and other community events. She has several characters she uses, but her favorite is Loveheart, a nice clown who always wins. "Ever since I was little I was fascinated with love," Heather says. "So I became Loveheart, because I wanted to make other people happy and let them know that they can do anything."

TAKE ACTION!

If you want to spread happiness to others who need it, ask your parents to help you find a convalescent home or a hospital nearby. You may also be able to serve at other places, such as a homeless shelter or an orphanage.

Then, contact the person in charge of managing and training volunteers. Some places have an age requirement to be a volunteer, so if you are too young, ask the person if you can at least set up some times to come and read, play games, or just visit.

FALLON TAYLOR

SHE KNOWS HER HORSES

Fallon Taylor of Ponder, Texas, was six years old when she first saw a championship rodeo on television.

"I can do that, " she told her mother. Now, at eleven, Fallon is the youngest member of the Women's Professional Rodeo Association (WPRA). Almost always in training, Fallon rides for several hours every day after school and spends almost every weekend on the professional rodeo circuit.

To become classified as a professional and a member of the WPRA, you need to have won two hundred and fifty dollars in professional competitions, and that means winning anywhere from one to nine events. From 1992 to the end of 1993, Fallon won enough competitions to make a total of $23,000. Much of that money is in the bank, but Fallon uses some to pay the entrance fees for rodeos and for her riding clothes.

Fallon races in the barrel event, a sport in which the goal is to ride a horse as fast as you can around several barrels set in a cloverleaf pattern. Racers can't knock any of the barrels over. It takes a great deal of skill

> "It lets me see things and places, and have feelings I'm sure I would not be having at my age."

and coordination. Fallon and her horse travel up to forty miles per hour, faster than in most other rodeo events. Of the eight events in the rodeo, barrel racing is the only one

in which women may compete.

Fallon's family owns thirty-two horses, and she has had to learn to ride many of them in case her own horse becomes ill or hurt. Dr. Nick Bar is Fallon's fifteen-year-old stallion and her best horse, although sometimes Pay Day Song, another favorite, is also a winner. "You have to know your horse," says Fallon. "If you don't click, you probably won't do very well."

Fallon spends several hours each day with the horses. She rides, races, trains, and just plain enjoys their company. The young rodeo star believes she's good at racing because she loves it so much.

"I love racing because of the great speed," she says, "and because you never really know what the horses are going to do."

According to her mother, Fallon is a natural with horses

73

and a beautiful sight to see when riding.

"She's all of seventy pounds, and her horse is twelve hundred pounds," her mother says, "but she has complete control of him." Fallon travels to rodeo events in a trailer with her parents and two dogs. Her rodeo schedule keeps the family busy, traveling year-round to the latest competition.

Fallon hopes to break the existing records in rodeo barrel racing. She wants to try to win the National Finals Rodeo. She's already raced at the Houston Astrodome, home of one of the largest rodeos in the United States. And she is the youngest person to compete in the Cheyenne Frontier Days Rodeo in Wyoming, considered the granddaddy of all rodeos.

Being in the WPRA allows Fallon to travel all over the country. And she believes her racing has taught her a lot besides horsemanship. "It lets me see things and places, and have feelings I'm sure I would not be having at my age," says Fallon.

When Fallon grows up, she wants to be a horse trainer. After all, horses are her best friends, and Fallon can think of nothing that she'd rather do than be around them her entire life.

TAKE ACTION!

When you're a kid, competing against adults can be scary and intimidating. They seem so much bigger and wiser. *Don't let them fool you!* Adults can be just as threatened by a talented ten-year-old. So, if you love doing something where the majority of participants are over eighteen, don't be timid. Get in there and show them what you can do!

DETRA WARFIELD
IT'S ALL ABOUT HISTORY

As a student in the public schools of Louisville, Kentucky, Detra Warfield had sat through what seemed countless hours of history and social studies classes. But it didn't dawn on her until she was a high school freshman that the history of African-Americans was studied *only* during Black History Month. Detra knew that, like her, almost half the students in Louisville were African-American. So why were there no African-American history courses at her school?

Detra called the local public school administration to find out. Not only were there no African-American history courses in her school, but there were no such classes in the entire system.

"I wanted to do something about this because it was important," says Detra. "There are many important black Americans in history, and we should be learning about what the black American experience was in history."

Detra realized that if she wanted to see anything change, she would have to meet directly with the Louisville school board. So she made an appointment to speak at the next school board meeting, which would include teachers, administrators, parents, and students.

After carefully putting her thoughts down on paper, Detra showed her speech to her friends at school and asked

> **"I knew I had to speak my mind and it would work out."**

them for their comments. She revised the text accordingly. Then every night for more than a week, she practiced her delivery in front of a mirror, or with her mother as an audience. Finally she was satisfied that the speech was perfect.

Detra included in her speech what she thought an African-American history course and textbook should be like. She spoke of the impact that black Americans have had in history and how important that history is to her. Her speech also conveyed how proud her ancestors make her feel.

"It was scary going up in front of all the people," she says. "I was shaking all over." But it was worth it, not just for Detra, but for the thousands of kids in Louisville who have a new course in African-American history. All nine high schools in Louisville now offer the class, and it's a good one. Detra has taken it herself.

"It is the ideal course," she says. "We read all sorts of books, see films, and have great discussions."

Detra is not sure why her speech was so effective, or why her words prompted action from the school board, which is sometimes not open to new ideas. Possibly, she thinks, it was because she was a kid talking about what kids need, and not an adult deciding what kids need. "I knew I had to do something," she said. "I knew I had to speak my mind and it would work out."

LINDA WARSAW

KIDS AGAINST CRIME

When Linda Warsaw was ten years old, her family's house was burglarized. Linda and her parents were not hurt, but they felt very angry and violated. Wanting to do something to lessen her anger and helplessness, Linda's mother began volunteering to work with crime victims at the San Bernardino, California, district attorney's office. At first Linda tagged along with her mother just for something to do, but it didn't take long before Linda herself got involved in the work.

Linda's mother worked with children who had been victims of crimes. She visited them in shelters, read to them, and played with them. To better understand their trauma, Linda *and* her mother read through many frightening transcripts of cases involving child molestation, kidnapping, and violence. Linda couldn't believe her eyes. She couldn't stop thinking about these kids and what they had gone through. She wanted to learn more so she could better understand and help young victims. She asked the district attorney if she could attend a real trial. By now everyone at the courthouse knew her, and he said yes.

The first trial Linda attended was that of a neighborhood baby-sitter accused of molesting a child. As Linda watched

> **"A lot of people won't do anything unless they get paid. But the real reward is just helping other kids."**

the child in the courtroom, something inside her changed.

"My stomach turned into a knot," she says, recalling the case. "I asked myself, How can children get victimized like that? Even as I was sitting there and hearing things with my own ears, I still could not believe that things like this actually happened." She decided then she was going to do something about it.

"I thought there needed to be a program to educate children to learn how to prevent these crimes and protect themselves," says Linda. A seed had been planted in the back of her mind, and one day, after witnessing another child abuse court case, all her ideas for a program came together. She rushed home to start writing a proposal. She called the program Kids Against Crime (KAC), and sent copies of the proposal to the director of the Victim-Witness Program, the police, the sheriff, and the people at the child protective service, a division of the city government that works on behalf of children and their safety.

Linda couldn't believe it when people started taking her proposal seriously— she was only twelve years old—but they were. They thought it was a good idea because its centerpiece was kids fighting for kids. The Kids Against Crime program became a reality. Nineteen kids attended KAC's first meeting at the local library. As membership grew, the mayor gave KAC an office at City Hall, and Linda became KAC's executive director. Today the group has more than 5,000 members, in groups throughout eighteen San Bernardino schools and in forty-five states throughout the country.

Kids from all races and economic backgrounds work on the program, teaching crime prevention in schools and at community fairs. They have even been trained by the police department to do fingerprinting, and have fingerprinted more than 25,000 kids in southern California.

Another feature of the program is a hotline for kids who need peer support. The KAC phones are staffed by kids, ages twelve to eighteen, who've undergone special training and are able to refer callers to professional help.

TAKE ACTION!

Are you interested in doing volunteer work? Ask your parents or teacher to help you locate an organization that needs your time and energy. Or contact Kids Against Crime and find out about how you can start a chapter in your town:

Kids Against Crime
P.O. Box 22004
San Bernardino, CA
92406

"Sometimes kids just need someone to talk to, if they are lonely, scared, or even if they just want to share some news," says Linda. "We're here for them."

Because of her work, Linda has won numerous awards, including the California Medallion for Service, the Young American Medal for Service, presented to her by former president Ronald Reagan, and the Presidential Volunteer Action Award, presented to her by President Bill Clinton.

"A lot of people won't do anything unless they get paid," Linda says. "But the real reward is just helping other kids."

INDEX

airplanes, piloting, 22-24
Andrews, Teddy, 6-8

bank, operating a children's branch, 17-19
Belanger, Kristen, 9-11
Bernstein, Daryl, 12-13
bicycles, restoring, 48-50
BIOtees, 30-32
Bookworm Network, 38
Brooks, Dwaina, 14-16
Burns, Andrew, 17-19
businesses, creating, 12-13, 27-29, 30-32

Caldwell, Tommy, 20-21
Carter, Rachel, 22-24
Children for a Safe Environment, 45-47
Children's Bank, the (Omaha, Nebraska), 17-19
clown, becoming a, 69-71
Connolly, Nichole, 25-26
crime, fighting, 77-79

Darwin, Charo, 27-29
designer, becoming a, 54-57

environment, working to save the, 30-32, 39-41, 45-47, 58-60, 61-63
Environmental Protection Agency (EPA), 25

floats, designing, 54-57
food, growing, 27-29
forest, saving a, 39-41

Golden, Casey, 30-32
Gomyo, Karen, 33-35

handicaps, overcoming, 42-44, 51-53, 69-71
Henderson, Aja, 36-38
history course, African-American, 75-76
Holleman, Andrew, 39-41
homeless people, feeding and helping, 6-8, 9-11, 14-16
horses, training and racing, 72-74

ideas, generating, 12-13, 27-29, 30-32, 54-57

Jalbert, Gina, 42-44
Johnson, Kory, 45-47

KAC (Kids Against Crime), 77-79
Kids F.A.C.E. (Kids for a Clean Environment), 61-63

lead, contamination of drinking water by, 25-26
Lebo, Justin, 48-50
library, running one's own, 36-38

McMullen, Jawauna, 51-53
Meier, Charlie, 54-57
Miller, Christian, 58-60
mountain climbing, 20-21
musician, becoming a, 33-35

pilot, becoming a, 22-24
Poe, Melissa, 61-63

Reid, Patrick, 64-66
rodeos, performing in, 72-74
running, middle-distance, 51-53

Sansone, Maria, 67-68
SAY YAY (Save American Youth, Youth Advocates for Youth), 6-8
science, studying, 25-26
sea turtles, rescuing, 58-60
sportscaster, television, 67-68
sports records and titles, 20-21, 42-44, 51-53, 64-66, 72-74
Strange, Heather, 69-71
swimming, long-distance, 64-66

Taylor, Fallon, 72-74
tee, golf, inventing a new, 30-32
tennis, playing professional, 42-44
Tournament of Roses, 54-57

violin, studying, 33-35

Warfield, Detra, 75-76
Warsaw, Linda, 77-79
water, lead contamination of, 25-26
wheelchair sports, 42-44
Women's Professional Rodeo Association (WPRA), 72
World Wildlife Fund, 60